THE INTERNET LIBRARY

The History of the Internet and the World Wide Web

Art Wolinsky

Enslow Publishers, Inc.

40 Industrial Road   PO Box 38
Box 398   Aldershot
Berkeley Heights, NJ 07922   Hants GU12 6BP
USA   UK

http://www.enslow.com

Books in THE INTERNET LIBRARY series

Communicating
on the Internet
Paperback 0-7660-1743-5
Library Ed. 0-7660-1260-3

The History of the Internet
and the World Wide Web
Paperback 0-7660-1746-X
Library Ed. 0-7660-1261-1

Creating and Publishing
Web Pages
on the Internet
Paperback 0-7660-1744-3
Library Ed. 0-7660-1262-X

Locating and Evaluating
Information
on the Internet
Paperback 0-7660-1745-1
Library Ed. 0-7660-1259-X

Library of Congress Cataloging-in-Publication Data

Wolinsky, Art.
        The history of the Internet and the World Wide Web / Art Wolinsky.
            p.   cm. — (The Internet Library)
        Includes bibliographical references and index.
        Summary: Traces the development of the Internet as a resource from
its roots in the late 1960s, as well as the growth of the World Wide Web
as a part of everyday life.
        ISBN 0-7660-1746-X (pbk)
        ISBN 0-7660-1261-1 (library ed.)
        1. Internet (Computer network)—History—Juvenile literature.
2. World Wide Web (Information retrieval system)—History—Juvenile
literature. [1. Internet (Computer network) 2. World Wide Web
(Information retrieval system)] I. Title.   II. Series.
TK5105.875.I57W64   1999
004.67′8—dc21   98-50684
                                                              CIP
                                                              AC

Printed in the United States of America

10 9 8 7 6 5 4

To Our Readers:
All Internet addresses in this book were active and appropriate when we
went to press. Any comments or suggestions can be sent by e-mail to
Comments@enslow.com or to the address on the back cover.

Trademarks:
Most computer and software brand names have trademarks or registered
trademarks. The individual trademarks have not been listed here.

Cover Photo: © Index Stock Imagery/Eric Kamp

Contents

Introduction

This is my friend Web. He will be appearing through-out the pages of this book to guide you through the information presented here and take you to a variety of Internet sites and activities. Web is also a reminder that there is always more to learn about the Internet.

The Internet is in newspapers and magazines. The Internet is on radio and television. There are Internet best-sellers in the bookstores, and there are Internet blockbusters on the movie screen. The Internet is everywhere you look, but how much do you really know about it?

When most people think of the Internet, they think of the World Wide Web. Web pages full of graphics, sound, video, and text are what most people consider to be the Internet, but it is much more than that. The Internet has been around for over twenty years, but the World Wide Web has been around for only a few years.

Do you know why the Internet was started? Do you have any idea how it works? Would you like to know more? I certainly hope so, because that's why I wrote this book.

You do not need an Internet connection to use this book, but if you have one, you can visit many of the places I suggest, and can extend your learning in ways only the Internet can allow. Throughout the book, I will be supplying you with URLs (uniform resource locators, which are simply Internet addresses) for more detailed information on topics covered here.

The Internet can provide you with answers to questions and give you hours of entertainment. It can also put you in touch with experts and can allow you to talk to people and learn about places halfway around the world. You may already know about the entertainment value of the Internet, but if you know how to use it as a learning tool, the Internet can help you get ahead in life. If you understand how it came to be and how it works, you will understand how to use the Internet most effectively.

Chapter 1

Before the Internet

In the 1950's, there was no Internet. The personal computer did not exist. All computers were large mainframe computers. They cost hundreds of thousands of dollars, filled entire rooms, and they were very complicated and very expensive to run. These giant computers were located in government buildings, large corporations, and universities.

You may be surprised to learn that the personal computer sitting on your desk is many times more powerful than these early monsters. You may even have a computer modem attached to your computer so that it can communicate with other computers, but in the 1950's, communication between computers did not exist.

▶ The Need for Communication

In 1957, something happened to make computer communication necessary. At that time, a great deal of tension existed between the USSR (former Soviet Union) and the United States. The countries were not at war, but the American people lived with an almost daily concern about the possibility of nuclear war. This period was known as the Cold War.

Everyone was concerned. Many Americans prepared for possible war by constructing fallout shelters. These sturdy underground structures were stocked with food, water, and other supplies to help their owners survive a possible nuclear attack.

The United States government was also concerned about the possibility of a nuclear attack. Some cities made community fallout shelters, and the government planned how to run a country that had just gone through a nuclear attack.

On October 10, 1957, tensions increased when the USSR launched *Sputnik*, the first space satellite to orbit Earth. The government decided that the United States must catch up with the technology of the USSR. One way to do that was to connect major computing centers around the United States so they could work together and communicate. The centers were to be set up so that messages could continue to flow even if one or more of the computers were destroyed by an attack.

Fallout Shelters:
Because of the threat of nuclear war, these signs were very popular in the 1950's and 1960's.

FALLOUT SHELTER

▶ The First Network Is Born

In the late 1960's, the Department of Defense and the Advanced Research Projects Agency worked together to create a network that would join super-computing centers. The result was the creation of ARPANET, the nation's first computer network. It linked four West Coast universities.

The nation's first computer network had many problems. First, the scientists had to figure out how to connect the individual computers. Take a look at Figure 1 on page 10. You are going to do some

Internet Addresses   Internet Facts   How Do I Do That?

To get more information on fallout shelters and a better idea of what the Cold War was like, you may want to visit the following sites:

National Reconnaissance Office
<http://www.nro.odci.gov/index5.html>
This site has information on Corona, the first Cold War spy satellite, and declassified spy images from space.

CNN Cold War
<http://www.cnn.com/SPECIALS/cold.war>
This site has original documents and interviews with participants of the era.

Cold War Museum
<http://www.coldwar.org>
This site has a trivia quiz and links to other relevant sites.

drawing, but please do not do this in the book. Draw four boxes on a piece of paper to represent the computers.

How would you connect them so that even if one or two computers were removed, the others could still communicate? Connecting each computer to the one immediately next to it will not work. That would form a square, but taking out opposite corners would leave the others without communication. Each computer needs to be connected to at least two others.

Connecting four computers this way *almost* does the trick. If we remove 1 and 4, 2 and 3 can still communicate. However, if we remove 2 and 3, the other two cannot communicate. The answer is that computers 1 and 4 need to be linked, but making all of those actual connections was not easy.

Do you see math coming into the picture? When

Figure 1

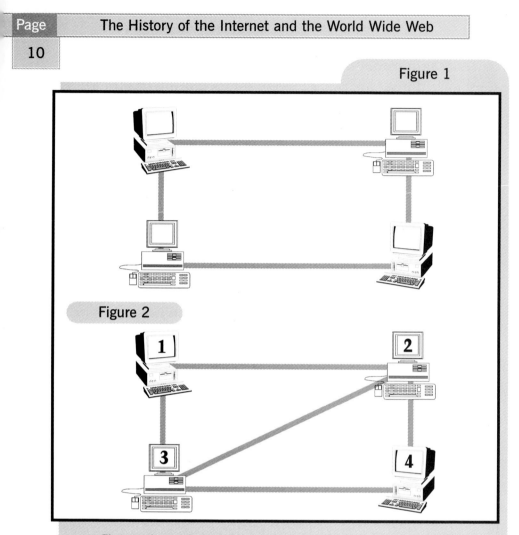

Figure 2

Figures 1 and 2 show how to connect four computers so that, even if one or two of them were removed, the others could still communicate.

you start connecting computers, you are dealing with lines, squares, triangles, and other geometric figures.

I drew the lines in Figure 2 this way because each of the four ARPANET computers was connected in more than one way, but not with all the possible connections. Look at Figure 2 again and see whether you can figure out why they were not all connected with multiple connections.

Math came into the picture when the plans were being drawn up, but geography entered the picture when the connections had to be made. Connecting the computers in California was not a problem. With the existing phone wires and heavy population centers, the connections were easy to make. The University of Utah, however, was another story. There were hundreds of miles of desert to go through and a little obstacle called the Rocky Mountains to cross in order to get there. Although connecting four computers may not be much of a problem, how about connecting forty, four hundred, four thousand, or even 4 million computers? Actually, it is not that difficult if you know the secret. Let's look at what it takes to connect five computers. Draw five boxes on a sheet of paper to represent these five computers. (Please do not write in this book.) Connect the boxes so that if some are destroyed, the remaining ones are always connected. (See Figure 4 on page 12.)

Figure 3

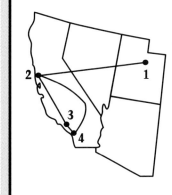

The Original ARPANET

1. University of Utah
2. Stanford Research Center
3. University of California, Los Angeles
4. University of California, Santa Barbara

Figure 3 shows the four computers that had to be connected in order to create ARPANET.

If you started by connecting all five in the shape of a pentagon, you are on the right track. From there the secret is triangles. Using triangles is just one way you can "grow" a network. Take a look at Figure 5 on page 13 to see how easy it is to connect three small networks into one larger one.

▶ Beyond ARPANET

ARPANET was a success. The government had a way of connecting computing centers to each other and of allowing scientists, university professors, and students to communicate and work together.

By 1972, the original four universities had grown to about fifty, but computers were not yet available to people in their homes. Computers were still kept only in major computing centers. The

Figure 4

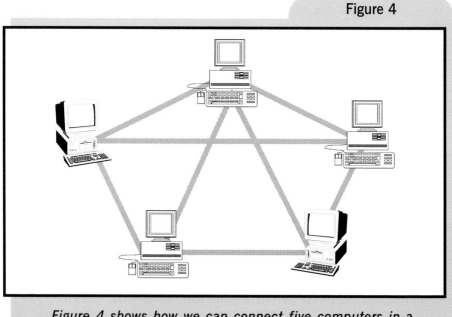

Figure 4 shows how we can connect five computers in a network by using a pentagon and triangles.

Figure 5

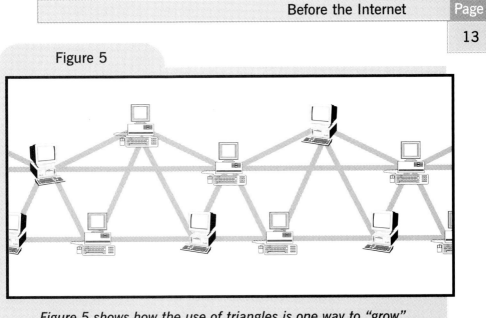

Figure 5 shows how the use of triangles is one way to "grow" a network.

people using them were all highly trained experts in their field.

Over the next ten years, as universities saw the success of ARPANET, other networks began to spring up. They had names like UUCP, USENET, CSNET, and BINET. Soon people started thinking about bringing individual networks together by connecting them.

Individual networks grew, but individual networks were made using similar computers. Getting different networks, with different computers, connected would be a difficult task. Scientists had to figure out how to direct the flow of information from one computer to another. They also had to figure out how to get different brands of computers to talk to one another. Finally, they had to figure out how to keep information safe and private. There were many questions to be answered and many problems to be solved.

Chapter 2

The Internet Begins to Take Shape

Just as people from different countries may speak different languages, computers have different operating systems. Computers with different operating systems cannot talk to each other unless there is some agreement about how that should be done.

▶ Controlling the Flow of Information

There had to be a way to make all computers talk to each other and to control the flow of information from one computer to another. People had to agree on a set of rules, called protocols, that all computers could use to send information back and forth.

Scientists came up with TCP/IP. You say it the way you spell it out (Tee-see-pee-I-pee). Transmission control protocol (TCP) tells computers how to break down and reassemble packets. A packet is a bitesized chunk of information. If a file is 100,000 bytes, the computer breaks the file down into many smaller packets of bytes. The size of the packets depends on a setting that is made on the two computers that are communicating.

Internet protocol (IP) makes sure each packet reaches the proper destination. Internet protocol or IP is an agreed upon way for all Internet computers to label and route information packets.

TCP/IP sets the rules for how information would travel across networks. The packet still had to be sent from one computer to another until it reached its destination. With so many possible paths to take, how could information get where it needed to go?

▶ Internet Traffic Cops

If someone on a computer in California wants to send a message to a computer in New Jersey, how can the information travel? In fact, the information may travel through a dozen or more computers before reaching New Jersey. It would be nice if we could use a straight path between them, but what if computers along the way are busy talking to other computers? What if one computer is offline? How will the information travel? Who acts as the information traffic cop? (A straight path would involve a smaller number of computers. Each computer that information passes through must process the information. Therefore, the more computers that are involved, the greater the time to process all the information.)

If we think of packets of information as cars, TCP/IP takes care of loading the cars, identifying the passengers, and setting the starting and ending points. Traffic is moved, in part, by Internet routers. Think of them as the Internet's traffic cops.

Routers are special computers that direct the flow of information. When information reaches a router, it sends the information to another computer closer to where the information needs to go. Look again at Figure 5 on page 13. Any computer can send information to at least three other computers.

In some cases, a computer can send information to four other computers.

When a router receives information, it looks at where the information is coming from, where it is going to, and what the traffic is like in the direction it is going. The router determines where to send the information by talking to other routers. Then it sends the information to another computer along the way.

Routers are even needed within networks. They direct the flow of information to and from each computer.

▶ Avoiding Traffic Jams

Think of information as vehicles. Some information is very simple and short. It can be thought of as a compact car. Other information comes in a large package, more like a slow-moving freight train. If you think of routers as intersections, the problem becomes clearer. Holding up traffic for one car at an intersection is no problem. Holding up traffic for a freight train, however, can cause a traffic jam. Scientists had to figure out a way to keep traffic flowing.

Getting information from one computer to another can be difficult, but the Internet directs the information traffic pretty quickly.

Another problem scientists were faced with was how to deal with the transmission of important information. Sometimes small pieces of information are very important. Think about an ambulance having to wait for other cars before it can get through an intersection. It would be even worse if it had to wait for a freight train.

▶ No Freight Trains on the Internet

The problem of large information packets versus small information packets was actually thought out before ARPANET. The solution is simple: Break up the freight train-sized information bundles and ship them in compact car-sized pieces. This process is called packet switching. Before information is sent from one computer to another, it is broken into small packets that will travel quickly. Each packet is numbered and contains information about where it came from, where it is going, and what type of information it contains.

When a router gets a packet, it sends that packet along toward its final destination. It may not send all packets along the same route. It is even possible that every packet will take a different route, but information is passed from computer to computer until each packet arrives at its destination.

Look at Figure 6 on page 18 and see what might happen when three packets travel from computer A to computer B, through router R.

Packet 2 takes the direct route, but the other two packets must pass through one or two additional computers before they get to their destination.

The router also looks at the type of information in the packet. Important information is treated as

Figure 6

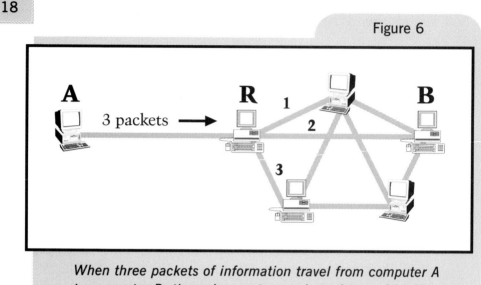

When three packets of information travel from computer A to computer B, through a router, each packet could take a different route.

if it is an ambulance and is sent through while other, less important information waits. Each packet contains information read by the router. The importance of information is determined by the type of information. For instance, e-mail and file transfers have different levels of importance. Computers and routers work in combination to determine what gets priority service.

The computer receiving the information collects packets as they arrive. They do not have to arrive in order. The computer will wait for all the packets to arrive before letting you know that the information has been received.

▶ Express Lanes, Checkout, Dealing Cards

Have you ever been the very first person in a line of people waiting for tickets to a concert or a sporting event. The many other people who lined up after you would have to wait. Well, waiting lines do not work this way on the Internet. If you know how your order is processed, you will understand why sometimes things move quickly and other times things move slowly.

Remember, when you request something from an Internet computer, it breaks the information into packets before sending it, but it does not always send all the packets at once. If one hundred people request service from an Internet computer, it does not necessarily serve them in the order in which they made their request.

Instead of handling the requests one at a time, like people waiting on a super-market checkout line, it is as if the cashier takes the first item from the first person in line, then takes the first item from the second person in line, then takes the first item from the third person in line, and so on, until everyone in line gets their first item to the cashier. Then the cashier starts taking the second item from each person in line.

Hang in There: Sometimes the Internet won't be running as fast as you want it to. Patience. Keep in mind that there are millions of people just like you trying to use the Internet all at once.

The computers work in a similar fashion, sending a few packets to the first person who requested information, a few packets to the second, and so on, until all of those who have requested information get some of it.

Suppose you requested a picture, Mary requested a word-processing document, and a hundred other people requested information from a computer. You would get part of your picture, Mary would get part of her document, and the hundred other people would get a part of their request. However, no one would see any of their requested information until all of the packets for their message or document had arrived at their computer.

▶ Getting Served Faster

The more people making requests, the longer the wait for computer information, even if your request came before the requests of others. So how can you speed things up?

One way to speed the flow of information is to do your Internet work when others are not doing theirs. In the United States, the two worst times to work on the Internet are from noon to three in the afternoon (Eastern Standard Time) and between seven and ten in the evening. At noon, all East Coast businesses are in full swing, and West Coast businesses are just opening and coming online. From seven to ten in the evening, people come home from work and dial in for their evening surfing.

So if you want to avoid the crowds, I suggest you get up early and avoid the "information rush." Getting online at two to three o'clock in the morning would do the trick, but I do not think mom and dad would appreciate that. You do need your sleep.

Chapter 3

Beyond the Machines and the Wires

In 1982 networks began connecting to each other using TCP/IP, and the term *Internet* was used for the first time. Until then, networks were isolated. They were like islands in an ocean. Though there were many other islands, people did not interact with the people on other islands, and each island had its own customs and rules of conduct. A network was mainly a way of connecting machines so that they could work and communicate together.

▶ Connecting People

As isolated islands, individual networks were limited in what they could do for people. As network connections were made, people began to exchange information, ideas, and customs. This powerful exchange of ideas and information between people in different parts of the country and the world gave scientists and educators powerful new tools for communication and collaboration.

Individual networks were about computers. The Internet introduced people into the mix. Once it became obvious that computers could help people relate to each other, the popularity of the Internet began to rise. People wanted to use it, but there were still obstacles.

First of all, only universities and government agencies had Internet connections. Even at that level there were problems. Using the Internet was not simple. In 1982, there were no Macs, no Windows computers, no mice, and no point-and-click menus. In order to use computers, you had to know a great deal about them. You had to spend a great deal of time learning the software.

▶ Talking UNIX

To give you an idea of what it was like to work with Internet computers in 1982, let's take a look at a simple operation today and then look at how the same operation was performed in 1982. Let us say there is a file I have named *junk.txt* that I want to delete, but I do not remember whether I saved it in a folder named *letters* or in a folder named *mystuff*.

Today, after logging on and going to my personal

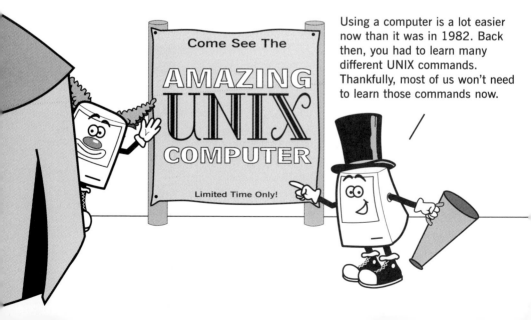

Using a computer is a lot easier now than it was in 1982. Back then, you had to learn many different UNIX commands. Thankfully, most of us won't need to learn those commands now.

folder, we might see a screen that looks something like Figure 7.

From here, I would use my mouse and double-click on the folder named *letters*. It would open, and I could look for the file. If it was not there, I would double-click on *mystuff*. With that folder opened, I could use the mouse to drag the *junk.txt* into the Recycle Bin.

It was not quite so easy in 1982. First of all, there was no mouse, and there was only text on the screen. There were no pictures. The concept was the same. I would log on, take a look at what was in *letters*, take a look at what was in *mystuff* and

Figure 7

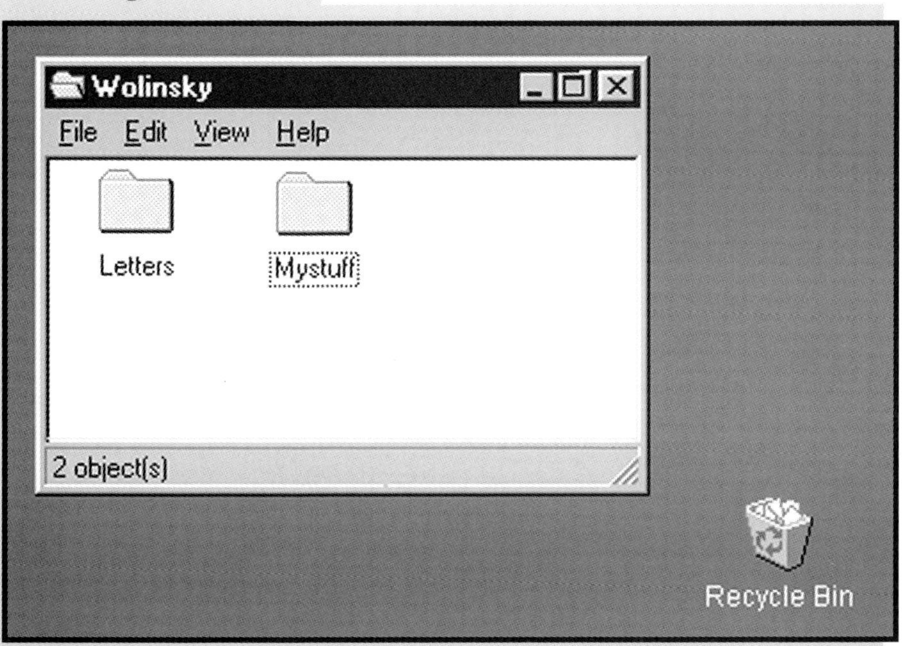

Today's computers make it easy to save information in a variety of folders.

remove the file. However, the steps I took to do this were more complex.

Most Internet computers in 1982 used an operating system named UNIX. (In fact, many computers still use this system today.) UNIX is complicated, so I'll just show you the series of commands needed to remove *junk.txt*. The box on page 25 shows a simplified version of what you would have to do.

First, you would move to the *letters* folder, (but they were not called folders in 1982). They were directories. The only thing you would see on the screen would be the name of the computer and/or the name of the directory. Each line on screen is a separate command that would have to be typed. After each command, either you would see a screen of information, or the command would be carried out without any visible difference on screen.

This is a *simple* UNIX operation. As I said, UNIX is still very popular today. Many system administrators (people who run the networks) need to be expert users, but the average user does not have to know anything about it. Aren't you glad?

▶ More to Learn

Certainly, UNIX was a challenge, but there was much more to learn than UNIX. Each piece of software that ran on the computers required commands, and each piece of software had its own unique set of commands. Today there are thousands of software packages on the market, and you may have dozens of them on your computer. Back then, there were not many software packages. If you

Internet Addresses | Internet Facts | How Do I Do That?

The series of basic UNIX commands needed to remove the *junk.txt* file is shown below:

computer> cd letters   (Move to the *letters* directory)

computer> ls-1   (Show what is in the directory)

computer> cd ..   (Move out of the *letters* directory)

computer> cd mystuff   (Move to the *mystuff* directory)

computer> ls-1   (Show what is in the directory)

computer> rm junk.txt   (Remove the file named *junk.txt*)

wanted to do anything else, you would have to write your own program.

Of course, this was not the whole story. There were other software packages and other things to learn. Some of the other software packages you might use had names like Finger, Ping, Archie, Veronica, Gopher, and WAIS.

There were many problems to overcome before everyone could use the Internet with ease. It became clear that the Internet offered a great deal to many people, but people did not have the time to learn the complex commands and software. People also did not have easy access to the Internet, because it was very costly to hook up to the Internet, and few people had hundreds of thousands of dollars to spend on a mainframe computer.

Up to this point, computers were in the hands of the engineers and scientists who built and used them. Over the next ten years, things would change

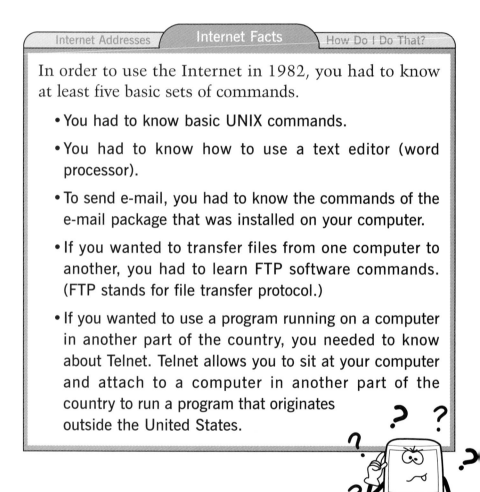

Internet Addresses | Internet Facts | How Do I Do That?

In order to use the Internet in 1982, you had to know at least five basic sets of commands.

- You had to know basic UNIX commands.

- You had to know how to use a text editor (word processor).

- To send e-mail, you had to know the commands of the e-mail package that was installed on your computer.

- If you wanted to transfer files from one computer to another, you had to learn FTP software commands. (FTP stands for file transfer protocol.)

- If you wanted to use a program running on a computer in another part of the country, you needed to know about Telnet. Telnet allows you to sit at your computer and attach to a computer in another part of the country to run a program that originates outside the United States.

For the adventurous among you, here are links to three different UNIX tutorials:

The Unix Primer
<http://bignosebird.com/unix.shtml>
A basic intro to Unix.

Idaho State University
<http://www.isu.edu/comcom/workshops/unix/>

Unix Tutorial for Beginners
<http://www.ee.surrey.ac.uk/Teaching/Unix/>
A more complete tutorial on a site from the University of Surrey, England.

dramatically. The first major step toward the future was the personal computer (PC) revolution. With the introduction of the desktop PC, nonscientists now could have access to computing power. Greater accessibility gave rise to the development of user-friendly software and a multibillion-dollar industry, but PCs still could not function as part of the Internet.

▶ Getting a Sense of Time

We have covered a lot of history and still have a lot to go. Let's take a look at what we have discussed so far. The chart on page 29 contains a view of some of the major events between the establishment of ARPANET in 1969 and the birth of the term *Internet* in 1982. The information is taken with permission from Hobbes's Internet Time Line.

During this same period, the number of computers with network connections went from 4 to 235. This increase may seem large, but look at what happened over the next ten years: From 1982 to 1992, the number of computers on the Internet increased from 235 to 727,000. If you think that is a jump, consider this: From 1992 to 1998, the number of Internet computers went from 727,000 to 29,670,000 and continues to grow.

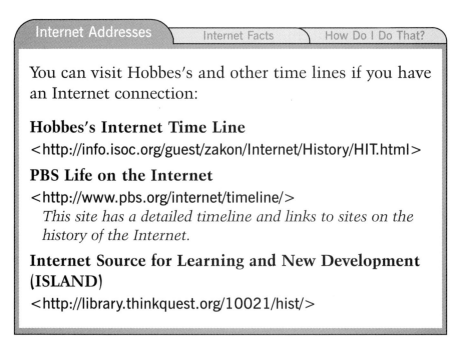

Internet Addresses   Internet Facts   How Do I Do That?

You can visit Hobbes's and other time lines if you have an Internet connection:

Hobbes's Internet Time Line
<http://info.isoc.org/guest/zakon/Internet/History/HIT.html>

PBS Life on the Internet
<http://www.pbs.org/internet/timeline/>
This site has a detailed timeline and links to sites on the history of the Internet.

Internet Source for Learning and New Development (ISLAND)
<http://library.thinkquest.org/10021/hist/>

Internet Addresses | Internet Facts | How Do I Do That?

Internet Timeline (1957–1982)

1957—USSR launches *Sputnik*, the first artificial Earth satellite. In response, the United States forms the Advanced Research Projects Agency (ARPA).

1966—First ARPANET plan is made.

1969—ARPANET commissioned by Department of Defense for research into networking. Four western computers are connected.

1971—ARPANET grows to fifteen sites. E-mail is invented.

1973—ARPANET connects to London.

1974—BBN opens Telenet, the first public packet data service (a commercial version of ARPANET).

1976—Queen Elizabeth II of England sends an e-mail.

1979—USENET is established.

1981—BINET and CSNET are established.

1982—TCP/IP is established.

Chapter 4

The Internet Starts to Grow

U p to this point, computer connections were strictly between the large mainframe computers. Individual users could not connect directly to the Internet. They could only connect to their own large computer. In 1983, all that changed. Desktop computers could now get on the networks.

▶ What's in a Name?

By the end of 1983, there were nearly one thousand computers online. Because each computer had its own address and managing so many addresses was difficult, specialized computers would be necessary to keep things organized. This need gave rise to domain name servers (DNS).

If you have an Internet connection, you probably have already experienced the frustration of not being able to contact a site and of getting a message saying, "The server does not have a DNS entry." Let me explain what that means.

Internet computers have two different types of names, one for humans to read and one for computers to read. Humans deal with words and computers deal with numbers. For example, <dune.srhs.k12.nj.us> is part of the Internet address you would need to reach the computer at Southern Regional High School. However, computers do not use that name. They use the numbers 198.139. 155.249, which make up the computer's Internet protocol (IP) number. Computers use IP numbers in the same way that people use home addresses.

Domain name servers are special computers that have tables of names and numbers. Every time a request using a name address is made, that request is sent to a DNS to see what IP number is assigned to that name. From there, the computers use the IP numbers to communicate.

When you get a message saying, "The server does not have a DNS entry", the computer is saying it can't find an IP number to match the name you typed. In most cases, you should check your typing. Either someone gave you a wrong name, or you typed something wrong. However, the computer may no longer exist, like a telephone number that is no longer in service.

If you get that same message everywhere you try to go, then it means you are having trouble connecting to the DNS. That might be a problem with your computer or with your Internet service provider (ISP). Figure 8 on page 32 shows what you might see in Netscape and Microsoft Internet Explorer when you try to contact a site that does not exist.

▶ Setting Up for the Explosion

At first, mainframe computer time was expensive and beyond the reach of the average person. The Internet continued to grow at a steady, controlled rate, however, as large corporations brought their computer operations online.

Then, in 1986, the National Science Foundation (NSF) funded the creation of NSFNET and five

Figure 8

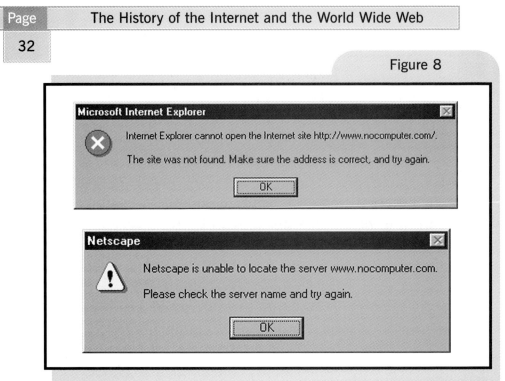

These are some of the messages you might see when you try to connect to a site that does not exist.

supercomputing centers to provide high-computing power for everyone. This government-funded effort allowed universities all across the United States to connect and provided the first explosive growth spurt in the history of the Internet.

By 1988, NSFNET had expanded to thirteen supercomputing centers, allowing access from many parts of the country. Between January 1986 and January 1988, the number of computers online jumped from just over two thousand to almost thirty thousand.

▶ Information, Needles, and Haystacks

With colleges and universities coming online, the amount of information available began to grow at an amazing rate. Early network users knew where to go for what they wanted, because they had either put it there or knew someone who had put it there. As the Internet grew, finding information was almost like looking for a needle in a haystack.

Universities created the problem of information overload, and universities also solved the problem. With access to the Internet, graduate students began to develop software to help locate information. They began to create tools that would automatically index information.

By now you have probably realized that the Internet is filled with acronyms (letters that stand for words that when put together form a new word)

Figure 9

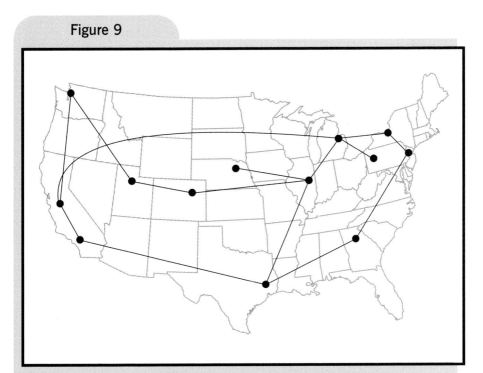

In 1986 the National Science Foundation (NSF) funded the creation of a network that allowed universities all across the United States to connect.

and names that have more than one meaning. College students also noticed, and they created humorous names for their new tools. A favorite comic book character of the time was Archie Andrews. Archie, together with his girlfriend, Veronica and his sidekick, Jughead, got into typical teenaged trouble.

It was not long before there were computer tools with these names. McGill University in Canada developed Archie, a sort of megalibrarian that visited other Internet computers and indexed files available to the public. If you needed to locate a file on the Internet, you visited an Archie server and made your search.

Most sources say the name Archie is a contraction of Archive, but I have also seen reference to the fact that the computer uses a search method known as the Andrews method.

Much later the University of Nevada developed Veronica, named after Archie's girlfriend. Veronica was short for Very Easy Rodent-Oriented Net-wide Index to Computerized Archives. (How's that for an acronym?)

The University of Manchester even created Jughead, short for Jonzy's Universal Gopher Hierarchy Excavation and Display.

▶ Gophers and Rodents

You may have wondered about the reference to rodents and gophers in the acronyms for Veronica and Jughead, respectively. No, the Internet is not infested with rodents.

The Gopher tool represented a major improvement in searching. The University of Minnesota

Internet Addresses   Internet Facts   How Do I Do That?

Conduct a search by using Archie at the following sites:

Archie Request Form
<http://theory.uwinnipeg.ca/archie.html>

If you want to find out more about the Archie comics, the only official site I know of is

<http://www.archiecomics.com>

You may find other sites out there, but they are not official and may be breaking copyright laws.

introduced it in 1991. Once again, college humor surfaced in the naming of the tool. The name Gopher was chosen because it was many plays on words rolled into one. It was a tool that burrowed through the Internet to bring back information. It was designed to go for information, and the mascot of the University of Minnesota was the Golden Gopher. Gopher was no laughing matter, however. It was a serious tool that was responsible for the next major jump in Internet use.

Gopher was the first really user-friendly way to search for information on the Internet. It made it possible to find information with almost no knowledge of computers. It did everything through a series of menus.

Instead of typing strange commands, seeing long computer path names and files, you would work your way through a series of menus. On the first level, you might see entries such as News, Libraries, Science, Math, and Geography. Selecting Science would lead you to a menu that might contain Biology, Chemistry, Physics, and other sciences. Selecting Biology would lead to another menu. Eventually, you would get to menus that contained articles dealing with the topic you had selected.

Gopher made it possible for anyone to find information on the Internet. As a result, unused computer terminals at colleges gradually began to see more use. Schools from kindergarten to grade twelve began to consider the Internet as a tool for research, and the University of Minnesota became a worldwide clearinghouse for Gopher servers that sprang up almost overnight.

The top-level menu from the University of Minnesota's Gopher is shown in Figure 10 on page 37.

Even though Gopher is no longer a popular tool for locating information, it is still around. You can even visit it by using today's Web browsers. No two Gophers are completely alike. Each one contains or points to information that was determined by the people who built it.

You can take a trip back in time and visit Gopher by using Netscape, Microsoft Explorer, or other Web browsers. On the address line, simply type either of the following:

<gopher://by067@freenet.carleton.ca/>
<gopher://gopher.ncf.carleton.ca/11/ncf>

These will take you to the National Capital Freenet Gopher in Canada. By selecting other Gopher and

Do I Look Like a Vet?
I'm tired of talking about animals. So, why don't we gopher some new kinds of information . . .

Figure 10

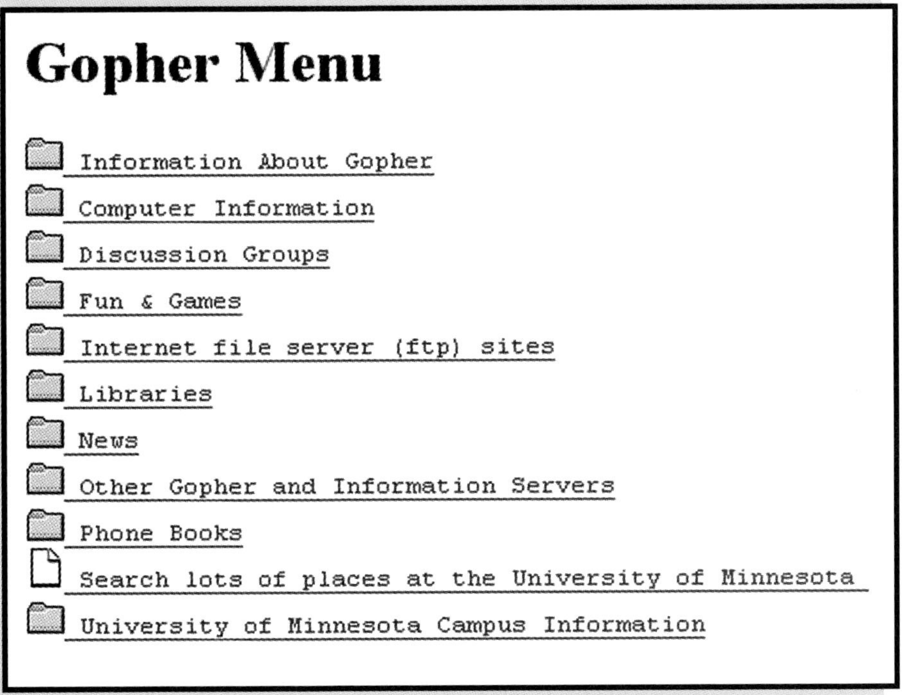

Gopher Menu

📁 Information About Gopher

📁 Computer Information

📁 Discussion Groups

📁 Fun & Games

📁 Internet file server (ftp) sites

📁 Libraries

📁 News

📁 Other Gopher and Information Servers

📁 Phone Books

📄 Search lots of places at the University of Minnesota

📁 University of Minnesota Campus Information

The top-level menu from the University of Minnesota's gopher is shown here.

information servers, you can visit all the registered Gophers in the world. Have fun burrowing through Gopherspace!

In the few years after it was invented, Gopher became *the* search tool of choice for Internet users. The number of computers on the Internet went from 376,000 in January 1991 to 727,000 in January 1992. However, Gopher was soon replaced by something that would revolutionize the Internet and lead us to another explosion that would be the biggest yet.

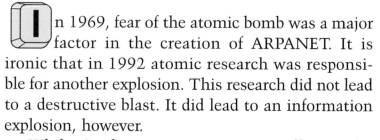

Chapter 5

The World Wide Web Is Born

In 1969, fear of the atomic bomb was a major factor in the creation of ARPANET. It is ironic that in 1992 atomic research was responsible for another explosion. This research did not lead to a destructive blast. It did lead to an information explosion, however.

While Gophers were popping up all over the world, the high-energy physics lab at CERN (Centre Européene pour la Recherche Nucleaires) in Switzerland, developed a piece of software known as the World Wide Web (WWW). It was designed as a way for scientists to communicate effectively. The WWW was unlike any Internet software yet developed. The concept was the same as today's WWW, but there were some major differences between the original version and the current version.

The original WWW did not have pictures, sound, or video on the screen. It did not use a mouse, and it was all text-based. What made it so revolutionary were its hypermedia capabilities.

If someone calls you "hyper," that person is probably referring to the fact that you have a great deal of energy, and you move around a lot. That is also a good way to describe hypermedia. If you were viewing a hypertext page in 1991, you would notice numbers next to some of the words. The numbers were actually programmed or linked to other pages somewhere on the Internet. Take a look at the following sample sentence from a page that might have been written in 1991:

```
After the Battle of Gettysburg (6),
Lincoln wrote a speech (7) that would
live in the memories of Americans
forever.
```

At the bottom of each page was a place for readers to type numbers or commands. If they typed the number 6, they might be sent to a page that described the battle. If they typed 7, they might be sent to a page that had a copy of the Gettysburg Address.

Did you notice I said, "they might be sent"? I said "might" because they were sent to a page selected by the person who created the Web page they were reading. People can make typographical errors or neglect to check links that may no longer work (because a document it linked to was moved, changed, or removed). The ability of anyone to create links to any Internet document was another reason for the explosion of use that took place.

A New Direction: In 1982, finding something on the Internet was very confusing. It's a lot easier for us now.

The numbers on the original WWW became known as hyperlinks. On today's WWW, hyperlinks appear in many forms. They may be colored or underlined words; they may be pictures; or they may be any spot on the screen that causes an action when you click with the mouse.

Up to this point in Internet history, if you created something, you put it on a computer, and people could search for it, find it, and use it. Suddenly people could not only put their own work on the Internet; they could link their work to the work of others and could put everything up in hypertext form for people to explore. Many people suddenly found they could become authors and publishers.

▶ The Gopher Lives

Over the next few years, Gopher continued to grow in popularity as a means of locating information on the Internet. The World Wide Web was gaining in popularity as well, but not as a means of locating information. There simply was not enough information available as hypertext documents to pose a threat to Gopher.

Even people who were creating Web pages used Gopher to locate the information they wanted to use as links in their documents. Web pages were a way of publishing, they were a way of expressing creativity, and they were a way for people to communicate on projects. All that began to change in January 1993, when the National Center for Supercomputing Applications (NCSA) released a new powerful tool called Mosaic. Mosaic was the first graphical Web browser. It was the forerunner of Netscape, Internet Explorer, and all the other Web browsers used today to view Web pages.

A mosaic is a picture created by combining small pieces of stone, tile, or other material. In this case, NCSA was attempting to create a single picture of the Internet by combining many individual pieces of software.

Up to this point, if you wanted to transfer a file from one computer to another, you needed FTP (file

Figure 11

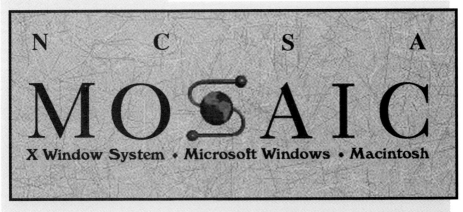

Mosaic was the first graphical Web browser.

transfer protocol) software. If you wanted to use a program on another computer, you needed Telnet software. If you wanted to visit a Web page, you needed WWW software. If you wanted to see a picture, you had to use FTP software to get it and another piece of software to view it.

Mosaic did all this and more. It delivered graphics and hypertext links to your screen and made everything accessible with a mouse. Now, instead of just seeing pages of text on the screen, you saw pages that looked as if they came from a magazine. There were pictures. You could click on words and move to other pages. You could click on pictures and move to other pages. It was nothing short of amazing.

In June 1993 there were 130 Web sites on the Internet. By June 1994, there were 2,738. By June 1995, there were 23,500, but that was just the beginning.

Internet Addresses   Internet Facts   How Do I Do That?

If you want details about the history of Mosaic, visit the following sites:

<http://www.ncsa.uiuc.edu/SDG/Software/Mosaic/Docs/
help-about.html>

<ftp://ftp.ncsa.uiuc.edu/Mosaic/Windows/Archive/
index.html>

<ftp://ftp.sunset.se/pub/www/Mosaic/Mosaic/Windows/
Archive/MosaicHistory.html>

▶ Business and the Internet

Up until 1993, the surest way to destroy your business was to try to promote it on the Internet. Conducting business on the Internet was unheard of. The Internet was strictly for science and academics. If you tried to do business on the Internet, you would be flamed. Flames are angry messages aimed at people who do inappropriate things or who do not follow the rules.

Don't Be Angry:
An angry message is called a flame. It is considered rude and inappropriate to send one to someone.

Before 1993, if you tried to do business on the Internet, people would not only refuse to buy your products, but also campaign against them.

In 1987 the NSF made a deal with IBM, MCI, and Merit Corporation to manage the Internet backbone, consisting of thousands of miles of wiring, thousands of routers, computers, switches, and other hardware. They managed the backbone during the growth years. As Internet traffic exploded, it was obvious to the NSF that the Internet could have important applications in all areas of our society.

It was also obvious the NSF would not be able to fund the improvements to the network and the new equipment that would be needed over the coming years. So in 1995, they built a new research network and turned the old backbone over to commercial Internet service providers.

The change basically removed restrictions against doing business on the Internet. It also made it possible for people to hook up to the Internet through their home computers. This home access was another major factor in the tremendous explosion that we know today as the World Wide Web.

The following graph shows the growth of the Internet before and after the introduction of WWW software.

Figure 12

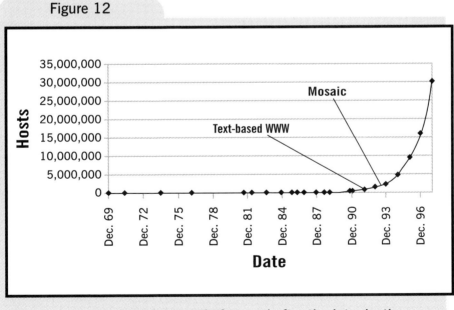

The growth of the Internet before and after the introduction of WWW software is shown here.

Chapter 6

The Gold Rush of 1995

T he Internet and the World Wide Web started to get a lot of attention on television and in the newspapers in 1995. People were becoming curious and excited about the new information superhighway. They wanted to get online.

People were able to hook up to the Internet through a local Internet service provider (ISP). These local ISPs began springing up all over the country. You can think of them as on-ramps to the information superhighway.

In the early days the path between your home, your ISP, and the Internet often seemed more like the Oregon Trail than an electronic superhighway. It may seem strange to refer to 1995 as the early days, but when looking at the problems of connecting in 1995 compared with the ease of connecting today, it is totally proper.

Today, generally all you do is pop in a disk from your ISP, click on Setup, make a few menu choices, and you are ready to go online. Way back in 1995, your ISP provided you with the method to get online, but you had to get the software and configure it. This usually took the better part of the day to get everything up and running, and then you could be sure there would be many hours of talking to technical support as other problems arose.

▶ Not All ISPs are the Same

You can get Internet access through an Internet
service provider (ISP) or a commercial information
service. The main job of an ISP is to provide access
to the Internet. They provide you with an e-mail
account. They often provide you with storage space
and the ability to set up your own Web site. A commercial information service offers many other
online activities and services not necessarily connected with the Internet. Examples of commercial
information services are America Online, Prodigy,
or Compuserve.

When you dial in to an ISP, you are connected
to the Internet. All you need to do is to start the
Internet software you want to use. If you dial in to
a commercial information service, you may first
have to go to the Internet area before getting on to
the Internet. How you do this depends on the information service you are using.

▶ Preparing for a Connection to the Internet

Before we take a look at the Internet today and what
it can do for you, I want to give you an idea of what
you should expect and what you should look for
when you want to get hooked up to the Internet.

Obviously, you need a computer. We could spend
a great deal of time discussing how to select the best
computer. There are no set rules or guidelines for
that. It is a matter of personal choice and finances.

If you are going out to buy a computer, do your
homework. Read magazines and talk to people.
Buying a computer is like buying a car. There are
different cars for different purposes. You would not

buy a convertible sports car to do off-road mud racing, or buy a two-seater for a family of five.

Knowing what you want to do and what you may want to do in the future can help you decide what to buy. If you cannot afford the biggest and best today, you may want to make sure you can make improvements to the computer's abilities in years to come.

Once you have the computer, you will need a few more items. You must select an Internet service provider or a commercial service provider through which you will obtain your connection to the Internet. You need a modem to connect your computer to your provider, and you need software to make the connection and do the things you want to do online.

Just a few years ago, almost everyone hooked up to their provider by using a standard modem and a regular phone line. (Of course, you could get a direct connection to the Internet if you wanted to spend thousands of dollars.)

A modem is a machine that hooks up to your computer and makes it possible for your computer to communicate with another computer somewhere else.

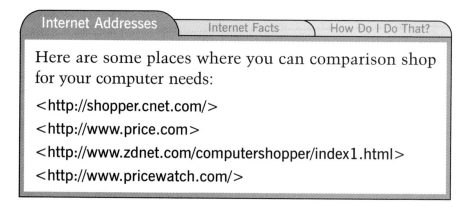

Internet Addresses   Internet Facts   How Do I Do That?

Here are some places where you can comparison shop for your computer needs:

<http://shopper.cnet.com/>

<http://www.price.com>

<http://www.zdnet.com/computershopper/index1.html>

<http://www.pricewatch.com/>

Today, there are different modems for different types of connections. There are ISDN (Integrated Services Digital Network) modems for special high-speed ISDN phone lines. There are cable modems that allow you to get Internet access through the same cable as your cable television service, and by the time this book is published, ASDL (Asynchronous Digital Subscriber) a new high-speed Internet service, should be commonly available through phone companies. Let's take a look at the advantages and disadvantages of each one.

▶ The Old Standard

Most people have dial-up connections to the Internet. They use their modem to dial in to the service provider and make the connection to the Internet. The speed of the modem directly effects how quickly you send and receive information. The speed of a modem is called the baud rate.

Many people think that *baud* means bits per second, but it is actually a measure of the number of transmissions per second—not the same as bits per second. If that is confusing, do not worry. All you need to know is that the higher the baud rate, the faster the modem, and the faster information can be transmitted and received.

In the past few years, modem speed has increased and prices have dropped. Many people, however, are still using slower 28.8 baud modems. (Note: 28.8 actually means 28,800 baud. You may

A Slow Beginning . . .
The first modems could only send things at a very slow rate, which made it feel like you were crawling slowly on the Internet.

also see 28.8K. The *K* stands for kilo, the metric prefix that means one thousand.)

Probably the most common modem today is the 33.6 modem, but 56K modems are becoming more popular each day.

You might think that faster is better, but that assumption may not be entirely correct. When two modems communicate, they can only function as fast as the slower of the two modems. Before you go out and spend money on a high-speed modem, make sure your service provider has modems at least as fast as yours. If you have a 56K modem and your service provider has only 33.6 modems, you can still communicate, but only at the slower speed.

Faster Than Ever:
Modems have gotten a lot faster over the last few years, so we can do things a lot quicker on the Internet now.

You may wonder how fast phone modems will get. Well, right now, they have reached and actually surpassed the speed limit set by the Federal Communications Commission (FCC).

There is another problem with differing speeds of modem connections. What would happen if you tried to travel at high speed down a highway filled with potholes? You would probably end up off the road more than you were on. The same is true of your phone line. Most phone lines have a certain amount of background noise. Noise affects your connection. If there is too much noise, you will lose your connection. The faster you want to connect, the quieter your line must be.

Fortunately, you do not have to determine what speed to use. Your modem will do it for you. When your modem first connects to another modem, it does something called handshaking. During handshaking, the modems exchange information to enable them to communicate efficiently. During handshaking, if there is too much line noise, the modems will slow down automatically.

If your service provider offers 56K service and you can afford a 56K modem, go for it. A 56K modem will communicate fine at slower speeds, and even if you have line noise today, things might improve tomorrow. If they do not offer 56K today, the provider certainly will in the future.

That's a quick look at standard modems. Most dial-up connections cost about $19.95 a month, but there is one more very important point to cover. Because you must dial in to your ISP, make sure the call is a local one. Internet charges are separate from phone connection charges.

Last year my service provider switched phone numbers, and I just assumed the new number was a local call, like the old number. The $749 phone bill I got the next month made it VERY clear that my phone connection to my service provider was a toll call.

▶ ISDN

ISDN stands for Integrated Services Digital Network. It is much faster than a standard modem, but the service is more expensive than standard service. With standard dial-up connections you usually pay $19.95 a month for unlimited use. With ISDN, you pay by usage. The more you use it, the more you pay.

ISDN is popular with businesses that use videoconferencing, because an ISDN provides a clear picture and allows phone data to travel over the same line. But ISDN has not yet gained popularity in many other areas due to the high cost.

▶ Cable Modem

If you have cable television, you might be able to get Internet access through your cable company. It will cost you about twice as much as a dial-up connection, but the speeds can sometimes be up to 100 times faster. Cable companies install everything and supply you with the special modem and network card for your computer. If you are like me and spend a lot of time online, the extra investment can be well worth it.

There are other advantages to a cable modem connection as well. With ISDN and standard modem connections, you must first dial in to your ISP to get on the Internet. Sometimes handshaking does not go well, and you have to hang up and try again. Sometimes you may get a busy signal. With a cable modem, there is no dial-up. When you start your computer, you are on the Internet.

Internet Addresses	Internet Facts	How Do I Do That?

Here are some places that can give you a more detailed look at modems. The links range from a comprehensive overview to an extensive look at modems.

<http://www.modems.com>

<http://www.modemhelp.com>

<http://www.modemhelp.org/>

▶ ASDL

Similar to a cable connection, ASDL has the advantage of always being on. There is no need to dial-up, even though you are using the phone line. You can also still make phone calls while you are surfing the net. Like cable, ASDL requires a special modem that is supplied when you sign up for the service.

The speed of ASDL is about fifty times faster than a phone modem. Pricing is higher than a standard connection, but usually lower than a cable connection.

The first ASDL service to the public was announced in April 1998 and was still not readily available early in 1999. As it becomes more readily available, standard dial-up connections will become a thing of the past.

▶ Which Is Right for You?

You may only have one service provider in your area. That makes your decision easy. On the other hand, if you are in an area that has it all, you must

Without a good Internet service provider, getting online would be as difficult as getting my family to sit still long enough to have breakfast together.

look at your needs and your budget in order to make a decision.

Regardless of how you connect, you want to make sure your service provider gives you the software and support you need to get started.

If you are searching for an ISP, here are some good places to start:

<http://thelist.internet.com/>

<http://www.internetnews.com/isp-news/>

<http://www.thedirectory.org/>

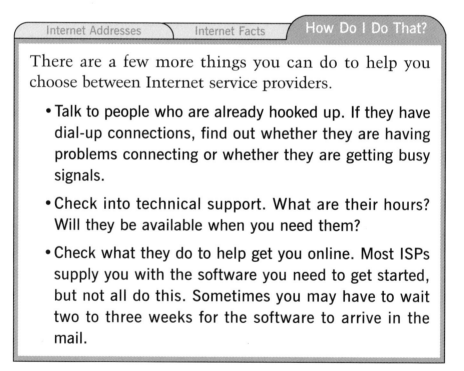

Internet Addresses   Internet Facts   How Do I Do That?

There are a few more things you can do to help you choose between Internet service providers.

- Talk to people who are already hooked up. If they have dial-up connections, find out whether they are having problems connecting or whether they are getting busy signals.

- Check into technical support. What are their hours? Will they be available when you need them?

- Check what they do to help get you online. Most ISPs supply you with the software you need to get started, but not all do this. Sometimes you may have to wait two to three weeks for the software to arrive in the mail.

Chapter 7

The Internet Today

Now that you know a little about the history of the Internet and about getting yourself online, it is time to look at what you can expect to find when you begin your online adventures.

You know the World Wide Web did not even exist until 1991, yet when people talk about the Internet, they think of the Web. One glance at the growth of the Internet since the invention of the Web explains why this is so. So what is the Web like?

The Web is like a library that contains millions of books that come to life with pictures, music, and video. It is like a mall where you can shop for things you want and for things you never imagined you would ever want. It is like an office where you can work with people from all over the world. It is like a club where you can meet and talk to people with similar interests.

It is for entertainment, it is for work, and it is for education. It allows you to interact with people from all over the world you would probably never meet otherwise. It allows you to travel to places you might never see.

Unfortunately, it can also get you into trouble that you might never encounter anywhere else. So before you go exploring, it is a good idea to know how to handle yourself. With millions of places to visit, not all are places you want to be. With millions of people online, not all are good, and not all are what they appear to be. If you ever feel uneasy about something you encounter online, talk to your parents or to another adult you trust. Let them know your concerns.

Let us take a look at your first experiences on the World Wide Web.

▶ How Do I Get There From Here?

We will assume you have set up an account with your service provider and that you are ready to get on to the World Wide Web. To do this, you need a piece of software called a Web browser. Remember Mosaic? Mosaic was the first Web browser. The people who wrote Mosaic started their own company and made the Netscape Web browser. They also made millions of dollars, but that is another story. Shortly after Netscape came out, Microsoft introduced Microsoft Internet Explorer (MIE). There are about two dozen other Web browsers, but almost everyone today is using Netscape or MIE.

When you set up your Internet account, chances are you were provided with one or the other with the installation disks. If you have Windows 95, MIE is probably already on your computer. So if your service came with Netscape, you have your choice. I will assume you are going to use either Netscape or MIE.

▶ Starting the Web Browser

Once you have made your dial-up connection and are ready to get on the Web, you will double-click on the icon for Netscape or MIE. When you do that, the software will start and take you to Microsoft's or Netscape's home page.

A home page is the first page of a Web site. Depending on how the site was designed, you can think of it as being similar to either the cover of a book or the table of contents (or a combination of both). On that page you will find links to other pages at the same Web site. You may also find links to other Web sites on the home page, but those types of links are usually on pages inside the Web site, not on the home page. After all, if you came to my house, I would not send you to my neighbor's house as soon as you came in the door.

Figure 13 on page 56 shows two samples of what you can expect to see. Your version of Netscape or MIE may look a little different, and the home page may have changed, but you will get the idea.

I do not intend to make you master of the Web browser. There are other books you can use for that. However, I would like to show you some features you can expect to find in any browser you may use. You should be comfortable with the basics, so you can explore the Web comfortably and productively.

▶ Understanding the URL Line

URLs are the way software knows where to go. There are three distinct parts to every URL. The following URL was designed to serve the needs of high school students. The URL is:

<http://www.srsd.org/studentlife/index.html>

Before we go any further, you may be interested in learning how you would read a URL out loud.

Figure 13

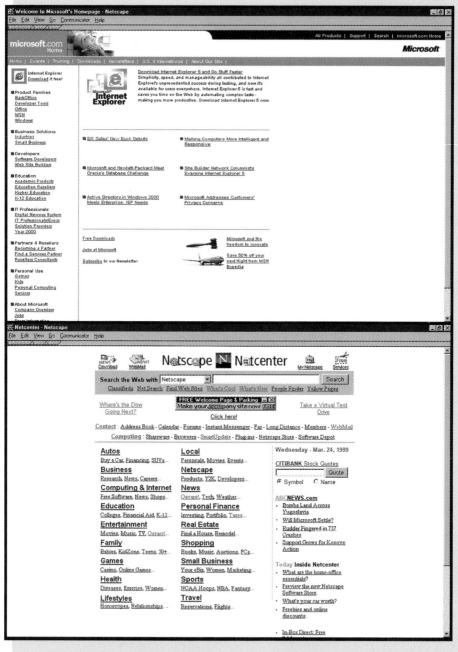

Microsoft's home page (top) and Netscape's home page (bottom) are shown here.

It is really very simple. You just spell it out and remember to read the : as "colon", the / as "slash" and the . as "dot."

There are actually two different slashes. The forward-slash looks like this /. The back-slash looks like this \. You almost always use the forward-slash with Internet URLs.

There are three distinct sections to every URL. The first tells Netscape what type of software operation to perform. In this case the *http://* indicates a WWW function.

Other possible entries would be *ftp://* for a jump to an ftp site, *gopher://* for a trip to a gopher, *telnet://* to attach to another computer, *wais://* to conduct a WAIS search at a specific site, or *mailto:* to send e-mail to a specific address.

The second section is the name and domain of the computer with the information being sought. The name is a series of two or more words separated by periods. In this case the name is *dune* and the domain is *srhs.k12.nj.us.*

The school chose the computer name, in this case *dune.* The *srhs.k12.nj.us* part was assigned to the school when the Web site was registered with the Internet.

The third section is a word or series of words separated by slashes. The slashes and words represent the subdirectories, or folders in the computer, and the file name of the information you seek.

In many cases a URL will end with *.htm* or *.html.* That word is the name of the actual file being retrieved. In our example, *www* is a subdirectory

Spelling Counts:
Be careful when you type in an URL. Make sure you spell all the words correctly and that you use capital letters when needed.

Some Common Controls

Take a look below at the close-up of the top of each browser. Above the browsers are short descriptions of each button.

1. **Back**—As you move from page to page on the Web, your Web browser keeps track of where you have been. Let us assume you have just visited ten different Web pages. You may move back through the ten pages in reverse order by using the Back button.

2. **Forward**—Once you use the Back button, you may use the Forward button to reverse the direction of your viewing. Another way to move to pages you have already visited is to use the Go menu. If you click on it, a list of previously visited pages will be displayed, and you can jump directly to the page you want, without having to go page by page.

3. **Stop**—This will stop the current page from loading. When the Stop sign is bright red, it indicates the page is actively loading. If it is gray, the page has stopped loading. There are times when you may want to stop a page from loading by clicking on the Stop button. One such time might be if you have been waiting a long time for something to happen and the screen does nothing.

4. **Reload/Refresh**—Sometimes a page does not load properly. Clicking Reload will start the process over again. Sometimes you may need to click on Reload to update information on your computer. For example, when you visit a Web page, your computer makes a copy of that page. The next time you visit, the computer can get the copy from your hard drive instead of from the Internet. This feature saves time and traffic. If a page has been changed since the last time you visited it, you may have to click on Reload to see the new information.

5. **Home**—When you first start your browser, it displays a page. This is called your browser's home page. Netscape

CyberU Search Page - Microsoft Internet Explorer

File Edit View Go Favorites Help

① Back ② Forward ③ Stop ④ Refresh ⑤ Home ⑥ Search ⑦ Favorites ⑧ Print Font Mai

Address http://dune.srhs.k12.nj.us/www/search.htm#hotbot ⑨

and Microsoft want you to see their Web sites, so they make them the home page on their browsers. The good news is that you can make setting changes so any page you choose can become your home page. If you set up your own Web site, you may want to set your browser's home page to your own home page.

6. **Search**—During the early days of the Internet, you would search for information using Archie, Gopher, and other search tools. Today there are many new search tools for you to choose from. The Search button will take you to a page at Netscape or Microsoft that will give you access to many of these new search tools.

7. **Bookmarks or Favorites**—As you visit sites, you will surely come to some sites you will want to visit again. The Bookmarks or Favorites button will allow you to create an electronic marker you can use as an easy way back to any site you want to revisit. All you have to do is click on the button and select Add to Bookmarks or Add to Favorites. It will add a link to the page that you can use by going to Bookmarks or Favorites any time you want to revisit the site.

8. **Print**—This button will allow you to print the contents of the page you are viewing. Be careful. It prints more than what you see on the screen. If the Web page you are visiting scrolls down the screen and is many pages long, it will print everything.

9. **URL Line**—This is a very important line to understand. URL stands for uniform resource locator. It is the way Web browsers locate information. What you see on the URL line is what the browser needs in order to find the page on the Internet. The URL tells the computer the address to go to in order to display the page or picture, play the sound, or do what it has to do.

or folder, and *search.htm* is the file that will be viewed.

▶ The End and the Beginning

You now know a little about Internet history, how to get online, and some Web browser basics. This book is ending, but you are just beginning an adventure of lifelong learning. Happy surfing.

See You Later . . .
Well, it's been fun, and we sure learned a lot about the history of the Internet. I can't wait to do some more Internet surfing! See you soon!

Glossary

acronym—A word formed by putting together the first letter of each word in a phrase. For example, the acronym for World Wide Web is WWW.

ARPANET—The joint effort of the Department of Defense and the Advanced Research Projects Agency that resulted in the nation's first computer network.

domain name servers (DNS)—A type of Internet address that uses words (rather than numbers).

hyperlinks—A method of accessing specific pieces of information from a Web site.

Internet protocol (IP)—An agreed upon way for all Internet computers to label and route information packets. Computers use IP numbers the way people use home addresses.

Internet service provider (ISP)—A commercial information service that provides Internet access for a fee.

mainframe computer—The predecessor to the personal computer. It was an extremely large computer that cost hundreds of thousands of dollars and filled an entire room. It was also very complicated and very expensive to run.

Mosaic—One of the first graphical Web browsers. It was the forerunner of Netscape, Internet Explorer, and the many other Web browsers used today to view Web pages.

packet—A bite-sized chunk of information on the computer.

packet switching—Breaking information to be sent via the computer into small packets that will travel quickly. Each packet is numbered and contains information about where it came from, where it is going, and what type of information it contains.

protocols—Rules that all computers use to send information back and forth.

routers—Special computers that direct the flow of information.

system administrators—People who run computer networks.

transmission control protocol (TCP)—Rules that tell computers how to break down and reassemble packets.

uniform resource locator (URL)—An Internet address.

UNIX—A computer operating system.

Further Reading

Computers and Children. Charleston, S.C.: Computer Training Clinic, 1994.

Henderson, Harry. *The Internet*. San Diego, Calif.: Lucent Books, 1998.

The Internet: How to Get Connected and Explore the World Wide Web, Exchange News and E-mail, Download Software, and Communicate On-Line. DK Publishing, Inc., 1997.

McCormick, Anita Louise. *The Internet: Surfing the Issues*. Springfield, N.J.: Enslow Publishers, Inc., 1998.

Mitchell, Kim. *Kids on the Internet: A Beginners Guide*. Grand Rapids, Mich.: Instructional Fair, 1998.

Moran, Barbara, and Kathy Ivens. *Internet Directory for Kids & Parents*. Foster City, Calif.: IDG Books Worldwide, 1998.

Index